Council of Europe
Archae

CW01510493

Conse
Patrimoine archéologique

Core Data Standard for Archaeological Sites and Monuments

Fiche d'indexation minimale pour les sites archéologiques

Cultural Heritage
Council for Cultural Co-operation
Council of Europe Publishing

Cover design: Graphic Design Workshop, Council of Europe

Council of Europe Publishing
F-67075 Strasbourg Cedex

ISBN 92-871-3816-8
© Council of Europe, April 1999
Printed in Spain

1. Core Data Standard for Archaeological Sites and Monuments

Contents

Preface

Between 1987 and 1992, as part of the Council of Europe programme created to support the European Convention for the Protection of the Architectural Heritage, a core data standard was prepared for records of architectural sites and monuments. In April 1993, the European Plan for Archaeology was initiated under the aegis of the Council of Europe's Cultural Heritage Committee, following the signing of the revised European Convention on the Protection of the Archaeological Heritage at Valetta, Malta, in January 1992, and in accordance with Resolution No. 1 of the 3rd Conference of Ministers responsible for the Cultural Heritage.

One of the five main elements of the European Plan for Archaeology consisted of a programme focusing on inventory and documentation techniques and standards in the field of the archaeological heritage. One of the principal features of this programme was the preparation of a core data standard for records of archaeological sites and monuments, to stand alongside that already prepared for the architectural heritage. A small documentation party was established to undertake the work.

CIDOC, the documentation committee of ICOM, was already in the process of preparing an archaeological data standard modelled closely on the Council of Europe's architectural data standard. The Council of Europe working party decided that the most practical course of action was to adopt the CIDOC data standard as the basis of its own standard, subject to some minor adjustments to reflect the narrower geographical focus of the Council of Europe. In matters of detail, there is little difference, and the document presented here is effectively that prepared by CIDOC.

The Council of Europe's core data standard for archaeological sites and monuments was discussed and endorsed by more than 100 delegates from thirty-two countries at a colloquy on The Archaeological Heritage: Inventory and Documentation Standards in Europe held at Oxford in September 1995.

The individuals and countries represented in the work of the Cidoc Archaeological Sites Working Group are:

Veletta Canouts (United States of America);
Nigel Clubb (United Kingdom);
Dominique Guillot (France);
Henrik Jarl Hansen (Denmark);
Roger Leech (United Kingdom);
Zana Kamberi (Albania);
Judy Marsh (Canada);
Irina Oberlander-Tarnoveanu (Romania);

Andrzej Prinke (Poland);
Gillian Quine (United Kingdom);
Trevor Reynolds (United Kingdom);
Stephen Stead (United Kingdom);
Elena Tashak (Russia).

The individuals and countries represented in the work of the Council of Europe Archaeological Documentation Working Party are:

Co-ordinating Committee:

Roger Leech (United Kingdom);
Charalambos Pennas (Greece);
Willem Willems (The Netherlands).

Members of the Working Party:

Martyn Barber (United Kingdom);
Roel Brandt (The Netherlands);
Dominique Guillot (France);
Henrik Jarl Hansen (Denmark);
Irina Oberlander-Tarnoveanu (Romania);
Jean François Van Regteren Altena (The Netherlands).

1. Introduction

1.1. Aims of the Core Data Standard

The documentation of archaeological sites and monuments plays an essential role in promoting the understanding, conservation and preservation of the archaeological heritage. Within Europe, a wide range of recording methods are employed in the compilation of inventories, often within a national framework. The compilation of these various inventories may have occurred for a variety of different reasons. However, some of these reasons enjoy a more widespread currency, in particular those relating to the protection of the archaeological heritage, and to providing some form of public access to the information held. The aims of this document are therefore threefold:

– to facilitate communication between national and international bodies responsible for the recording and protection of the archaeological heritage;

– to assist countries at an early stage in developing systems for the recording and protection of the archaeological heritage;

– to facilitate research utilising archaeological core data where this has an international dimension.

In the form presented here, the core data standard for archaeological sites has retained a close relationship to that already prepared for architectural sites and monuments by the Council of Europe (Council of Europe 1995). This should be advantageous to countries able or wishing to include within one database information relating to all periods of human history. Furthermore, this standard can also be linked with a working standard prepared by CIDOC for archaeological objects (CIDOC 1992), and with the CIDOC minimum data standard for museum objects (CIDOC 1995), which includes archaeological objects.

1.2. Using the Core Data Standard

The various sections into which the data standard is divided represent the minimum categories of information required in order to make a reasonable assessment of a monument or site, whether for planning, management, academic, or other purposes. In addition, allowance is made for reference to be provided to further information held in databases, document centres and elsewhere which may be necessary for the detailed understanding and care of individual monuments or sites or categories of monument or site.

The mandatory sections within the data standard provide for a minimum amount of information required for indexing in structured fields and describing in free text fields an archaeological monument or site. The optional sections, sub-sections and fields allow for the recording of particular aspects of a monument or site in greater detail. For example, a site may be cross-referenced to a larger complex of which it forms part, or to records of excavations undertaken on the site. Cross-referencing can also be made to more detailed documentary information either held by or known to the organisation responsible for the particular monument or site record. Clearly the actual level and detail of recording undertaken by individual organisations will vary according to its own requirements and resources.

Not all the sections are mandatory. Each section contains a varying number of sub-sections, some of which are mandatory, that is, the information must be recorded, while others are optional – recording of information depends upon the priorities of the recording organisation. Alternatively, of course, the information may not exist. For example, there may never have been an excavation undertaken at a particular site, in which case sub-section 2.1.8. cannot be completed.

While many of the sub-sections are optional, once it has been decided to record the type of information they refer to, then some or all of the fields within the sub-section become mandatory. For example, if it is decided to make cross-reference to records of archaeological excavations/events (sub-section 2.1.8), then the reference number of that excavation record and the name of the organisation responsible for curating that record must be entered.

The individual sections within the core data standard are as follows:

– Section 1 identifies the monument or site, and allows cross-referencing to records of events, for example, excavation and/or survey undertaken at that site, and to records of artefactual and archival material associated with the site;

– Section 2 locates the monument or site in terms of address, political, cartographic and other spatial criteria;

– Section 3 describes the type of monument or site being recorded;

– Section 4 allows for a date to be assigned to a monument or site, or for dates to be assigned to particular phases of use;

– Section 5 records the physical condition of the monument or site;

– Section 6 permits a note to be made of any form of protection, legislative or otherwise, which applies to the monument or site;

– Section 7 provides for a brief summary of what is known, archaeologically, about the monument or site.

Although many of the entry fields within the sections and sub-sections require only a single piece of information (designated "unique" within the data standard), it is recognised that in certain instances two or more terms may be relevant to a particular monument or site within a single field, sub-section or section. For example, an archaeological site may straddle the border of two adjacent administrative areas, or more than one excavation may have taken place at a particular site. In such instances, the data standard recommends the repetition of the whole sub-section or section rather than "multiple entry" within one field. Thus, in cases where more than one excavation has occurred at a particular site, each would be treated as a separate event and all of the cross-references in 2.1.8 would be repeated for each excavation record.

1.3. Implementing the Core Data Standard

The core data standard presented here has been devised within a theoretical framework which can be employed in both manual and computer-based systems. Organisations proposing to implement the data standard are likely to build on the data standard and its theoretical framework to meet their own recording needs. The theoretical framework which lies behind the construction of this data standard is more fully explained in the CIDOC document, and only a brief summary is presented here.

Clearly the need to maintain a close relationship to the existing data standard for the architectural heritage has placed certain restrictions on the format and content. However, the standard prepared by CIDOC draws much from the practical experience of organisations who have already implemented heritage databases, for example, DKC, Denmark; MONARCH, England; DRACAR, France; and ARCHIS, the Netherlands.

An important element of the data standard, and of archaeological databases, is the means by which the various sections are linked. The relationship between different categories of information is as important as those individual categories of information themselves. Thus within any database implementing the data standard presented here, all sections would need to be connected to section 2.1., which identifies the monument or site, names the source of the record, and provides the date on which the record was compiled. However, in addition other sections need to be closely linked to each other. For example, there is a clear need for a particularly close relationship to be established between section 2.3 (Type) and section 2.4 (Dating) in order to allow explicit links to be made between monument or site type and period for multi-period monuments or sites whose character has changed through time, for example, enclosed settlement/Bronze Age; open settlement/Iron Age; villa/Roman.

1.4. The future of the Core Data Standard

The core data standard presented here is intended as a guide. Different organisations in different countries record archaeological information for different reasons and to varying degrees of detail. For this reason, a number of the sections, sub-sections and fields are optional rather than mandatory, in order to allow different organisations to record to a level appropriate to their aims and resources.

The Council of Europe would welcome comments on this data standard, particularly from those who gain practical experience of implementing it as part of their own heritage database. The Council of Europe wishes the wording of its own archaeological data standard to remain the same as the standard prepared by CIDOC, on which this document is based. Therefore the Council of Europe proposes to maintain close liaison with CIDOC over the future development of the standard. All comments received by the Council of Europe will be forwarded to CIDOC for consideration, and the Council of Europe intends to adopt any material alterations to the data standard which may arise from such comments and which are relevant to Europe.

1.5. Contact for comments

Dr Roger Leech, Royal Commission on the Historical Monuments of England, National Monuments Record Centre, Kemble Drive, Swindon SN2 2GZ, United Kingdom.

2. The Core Data Standard

The following presents the definitions of the sections, sub-sections and fields contained within the Core Data Standard. Some of these are mandatory. Others are optional and the need to complete them will vary according to the nature of the record held and to the individual organisational requirements:

2.1. Names and references

This is a mandatory section which identifies the monument or site.

2.1.1. Reference number

The number or combination of characters which uniquely identifies each monument or site recorded by the organisation within its database, for example, 615649.

(Alphanumeric, unique, mandatory)

2.1.2. Name of monument or site

A free-text field which records the name or names by which a monument or site was or is known, for example, Stonehenge.

(Alphanumeric, unique, optional)

2.1.3. Date of compilation and date of last update

This sub-section records the date of compilation of the site or monument record, and the date on which that recorded was last amended.

2.1.3.1. Date of compilation

The date on which the core record was created. Use of the ISO standard for the date is recommended, for example, 1986-06-22.

(Alphanumeric, unique, mandatory)

2.1.3.2. Date of last update

The date on which the monument or site record was last added to, altered, or amended. This date will be modified whenever the record is updated. Use of the ISO standard for the date is recommended, for example, 1993-07-12.

(Alphanumeric, unique, mandatory)

2.1.4. Originator of reference

The name of the individual or organisation responsible for curating the monument or site record. This information is useful in establishing the provenance of the record when data is exchanged between recording organisations, for example, RCAHMW.

(Alphanumeric, unique, mandatory)

2.1.5. Cross reference to related records of monuments or sites

This sub-section enables cross-referencing to records of related monuments or sites. For example, relating a record to its wider complex record, for example, a house within a settlement. It is optional and can be repeated.

2.1.5.1. Reference number

The number or combination of characters which uniquely identifies each related record, for example, SM97342.

(Alphanumeric, unique, mandatory)

2.1.5.2. Qualifier of relationship

The qualifier indicates the type of relationship between one record and another, such as a hierarchical "parent-child" relationship linking an archaeological complex and an individual site. The entry will be one of the following: "part of", "contains", or "related to". In the example of a record for a house, the relationship to a settlement would be "part of". In the record for the settlement, the relationship to the house would be "contains". The house could also be "related to" another house within the same settlement.

(Alphanumeric, unique, mandatory)

2.1.5.3. Originator of reference

The name of the individual or organisation responsible for curating the related record, for example, the Ministry of Culture.

(Alphanumeric, unique, mandatory)

2.1.6. Cross reference to archaeological collections and artefacts

This sub-section enables cross-referencing to related records of archaeological collections. It is optional and can be repeated.

2.1.6.1. Reference number

The number or combination of characters which uniquely identifies each related collection or artefact record, for example, 57486.

(Alphanumeric, unique, mandatory)

2.1.6.2. Originator of reference

The name of the individual or organisation responsible for curating the related record, for example, Nationalmuseet (DKC).

(Alphanumeric, unique, mandatory)

2.1.7. Cross reference to documentation

This sub-section enables cross-referencing to the published and unpublished documentation associated with the site or monument. It is optional and can be repeated.

2.1.7.1. Reference number

The number or combination of characters which uniquely identifies each related piece of documentation, for example, DD27483.

(Alphanumeric, unique, mandatory)

2.1.7.2. Type of documentation/archive

The type of documentation or archive associated with the site. Controlled vocabulary is desirable, for example, photographic, graphic, unpublished text, bibliographic, electronic, cartographic.

(Alphanumeric, unique, mandatory)

2.1.7.3. Originator of reference

The name of individual or organisation responsible for curating the related documentation record, for example, Royal Commission on the Historical Monuments of England.

(Alphanumeric, unique, mandatory)

2.1.8. Cross reference to archaeological events

This sub-section makes it possible to relate, for example, records of archaeological excavations or surveys to those of the monument or site. Where multiple events have occurred at a monument or site, for example, a survey followed by excavation, separate entries in this sub-section should be completed. It is an optional sub-section which can be repeated.

2.1.8.1. Reference number

The number or combination of characters which uniquely identifies each related event record, for example, CX974\38.

(Alphanumeric, unique, mandatory)

2.1.8.2. Type of event

The nature of the event, for example, excavation, survey. Where multiple events have occurred, each should have a separate entry.

(Alphanumeric, unique, mandatory)

2.1.8.3. Start date of recording event

The date on which the recording event commenced. Use of the ISO standard for date is recommended, for example, 1896-06-24.

(Alphanumeric, unique, optional)

2.1.8.4. End date of recording event

The date on which the recording event terminated. Use of the ISO standard for date is recommended, for example, 1896-07-30.

(Alphanumeric, unique, optional)

2.1.8.5. Originator of reference

The name of the individual or organisation responsible for curating the related event record, for example, the Department of Environmental Affairs and Tourism.

(Alphanumeric, unique, optional)

2.2. Location

This is a mandatory section which defines the spatial location of the monument or site in terms of political, postal, geographic and cartographic criteria.

Any combination of sub-sections defined below may be employed to identify the location of the monument or site. More than one type of sub-section may be used to more closely define the location or to make otherwise ambiguous locations more precise. It should be noted that at least one sub-section must be used, but that no individual sub-section is mandatory.

2.2.1. Administrative location

This is an optional sub-section for details of administrative location. It can be repeated.

2.2.1.1. Country or nation

The name of the country or nation within which the monument or site is located, for example, France.

(Alphanumeric, unique, optional (mandatory for exchanging data with other countries))

2.2.1.2. Geo-political unit

This is used for recording the geographical or political subdivisions of countries or nations within which the monument or site is located; for instance *régions* in France, *Länder* in Germany, counties in Great Britain.

(Alphanumeric, unique, mandatory)

2.2.1.3. Administrative sub-division

This is used for recording the further administrative sub-divisions appropriate to the monument or site. According to the administrative structure of each nation or country, a number of repeat entries in this field may be required. For example, in Great Britain England is further subdivided into county, district and parish, therefore Wiltshire, Salisbury and Amesbury would require three entries.

(Alphanumeric, unique, mandatory)

It should be noted that it is essential to differentiate between the different levels of administrative sub-divisions which relate to each site or monument, for example, local or regional.

2.2.2. Site location

This is an optional sub-section which provides for a free-text explanation of the location of the site or monument.

2.2.2.1. Description of location

A free text field enabling a short description of the location of a monument or site to be recorded, to assist identification in the field, and to provide a more precise location for sites in sparsely populated or poorly-mapped areas.

(Alphanumeric, unique, mandatory)

2.2.3. Address

This enables the recording of the location of monuments or sites which have a postal address, especially those within built-up areas. It is an optional sub-section and can be repeated, for example if the monument or site is located on two streets or has two postal names. All the fields are optional but at least one must be completed.

2.2.3.1. Name for address purposes

Use this field to record the name of the monument or site for address purposes (or postal name), for example, Cruive Cottage.

(Alphanumeric, unique, optional)

2.2.3.2. Number in the street or road

Use this field for the number of the monument or site in the street or road, for example, 27A.

(Alphanumeric, unique, optional)

2.2.3.3. Name of street or road

Use this field for the name of the street or road, for example, Calea Victoriei.

(Alphanumeric, unique, optional)

2.2.3.4. Locality

Use this field for commonly known non-administrative units such as hamlets and townships, for example, Pincevent.

(Alphanumeric, unique, optional)

2.2.3.5. Town or city

Use this field for the name of the town or city, for example, Stockholm.

(Alphanumeric, unique, optional)

2.2.3.6. Postal or other similar national address code

Use this field to record an address code, for example, 67000, K1A 0C8.

(Alphanumeric, unique, optional)

2.2.4. Cadastral reference/Land unit

Some countries operate a system of allocating reference numbers to individual blocks or units of land. The land unit reference number relevant to the particular monument or site can be entered here. This field is optional and can be repeated.

2.2.4.1. Cadastral reference

This field enables cross reference to the land unit or parcel(s) current in some nations or countries, for example, block reference 941\278.

(Alphanumeric, unique, mandatory)

2.2.5. Cartographic reference

This is an optional sub-section used to record the two- or three-dimensional spatial co-ordinates required for locating the monument or site within the mapping system(s) used by individual countries or nations. The four fields 2.2.5.5-8 should be repeated for each set of co-ordinates.

2.2.5.1. Cartographic identifier

The identifier of the cartographic entity where the monument or site has more than one such entity related to it, for example, polygon 1.

(Alphanumeric, unique, optional)

2.2.5.2. Spatial referencing system

This field specifies the spatial or cartographic referencing system employed, for example, UTM, Lambert, GPS, Ordnance Survey.

(Alphanumeric, unique, mandatory)

2.2.5.3. Topology

This field specifies whether the spatial co-ordinates given relate to a point, line or area, for example, P, L, A.

(Alphanumeric, unique, mandatory)

2.2.5.4. Qualifier

This field allows for an indication of the significance and reliability of the cartographic or spatial co-ordinates for a site or monument, for example, approximate, centre. Controlled vocabulary is desirable.

(Alphanumeric, unique, mandatory)

The following four fields should be repeated for each co-ordinate.

2.2.5.5. Sequence number

When an archaeological site or monument is of linear or polygonal shape, it is advisable to list a series of sets of co-ordinates describing its course rather than a single reference to, for example, its central point. These should be listed in sequence. The sequence number for each set of co-ordinates should be entered here. For example 1 for a point, 1,2... for a line and 1,2,3... for a polygon.

(Alphanumeric, unique, mandatory)

2.2.5.6. Z-co-ordinate

Value or identifier of cartographic reference. It locates a record in relation to a vertical datum, for example, 30 metres above sea-level, 30 metres below chart datum for underwater sites.

(Alphanumeric, unique, optional)

2.2.5.7. X-co-ordinate

Value or identifier of cartographic reference. This is normally the east-west co-ordinate.

(Numeric, unique, mandatory)

2.2.5.8. Y-co-ordinate

Value or identifier of cartographic reference. This is normally the north-south co-ordinate.

(Numeric, unique, mandatory)

2.3. Type

This section allows for the indexing of a monument or site according to functional or descriptive criteria. An entry is mandatory and must be linked to an entry in section 2.4 (Dating), for example, villa/Roman. Controlled vocabulary is necessary and should include "unknown". This section can be repeated to accommodate changes in type at a monument or site through time.

2.3.1. Monument or site type

The term by which a monument has been indexed. This will normally be the interpretation of the monument by functional or descriptive criteria, for example, villa; linear earthwork. Controlled vocabulary is desirable.

(Alphanumeric, unique, mandatory)

2.3.2. Monument or site category

Broad functional or descriptive category to which the type belongs, for example, residential. Controlled vocabulary is desirable. Note that if a hierarchical thesaurus is being used this field may not be required.

(Alphanumeric, unique, optional)

2.4. Dating

This is a mandatory section allowing for the recording of precise dating when it is known, or date ranges or periods when it is imprecise. This section can be repeated. An entry in this section should be linked to one in section 2.3.

Sub-section 2.4.1. is mandatory but one or more of the optional sub-sections which follow it may be employed to define the dating more closely.

2.4.1. Cultural period

This is a mandatory sub-section allowing for the indexing of a site or monument according to the cultural period to which it has been assigned.

2.4.1.1. Cultural period

The cultural period to which the monument or site, or a part or phase of the monument or site, belongs; for example, Neolithic. A controlled vocabulary is desirable and must include "unknown".

(Alphanumeric, unique, mandatory)

2.4.2. Century

This is an optional sub-section for recording the century to which the site or monument, or a part of it, belongs.

2.4.2.1. Century

The century of the monument or site, for example, 17th century. This field is only appropriate for monuments or sites which belong to historic periods.

(Alphanumeric, unique, mandatory)

2.4.3. Date range

This is an optional sub-section for recording the date range which encompasses the use of the monument or site, or a particular phase of activity at the monument or site.

2.4.3.1. From date

The earliest date in the range, for example, 1640.

(Alphanumeric, unique, mandatory)

2.4.3.2. To date

The latest date in the range, for example, 1660.

(Alphanumeric, unique, mandatory)

2.4.4. Scientific and absolute dates

This is an optional sub-section which enables a more precise date to be recorded from sources such as documentary evidence, inscriptions, radiocarbon dates and dendrochronological dates.

2.4.4.1. Date

The scientific or absolute date associated with the monument or site, for example, 1580-1410 Cal BC (HAR-1234).

(Alphanumeric, unique, mandatory)

2.4.4.2. Method

This indicates the method by which the date was derived, for example, Carbon 14, dendrochronology. A controlled vocabulary is desirable.

(Alphanumeric, unique, mandatory)

2.5. Physical condition

This section is used to record the physical condition of the monument or site and the date of assessment. It is optional and can be repeated. It may be useful for the continued assessment of the management of the monument or site to maintain entries in this section over time. This will enable damage or deterioration to be logged. It may also be necessary to include additional fields to record management details, depending on the functions of the recording organisation.

2.5.1. Condition

This field records the physical integrity of the monument or site, for example, intact, destroyed, restored, unknown, and so on. A controlled vocabulary is desirable.

(Alphanumeric, unique, mandatory)

2.5.2. Date condition assessed

The date on which the condition was assessed. This field is optional because many condition reports in the past may not have been dated. Use of the ISO standard for date is recommended, for example, 1994-10-27.

(Alphanumeric, unique, optional)

2.6. Designation/Protection status

This is an optional section allowing for a statement on whether the monument or site is designated or protected and if so the type of designation or protection and the date at which it was granted. This section can be repeated.

2.6.1. Type of designation or protection

This denotes the designation or protection category. A controlled vocabulary is desirable, for example, municipal, provincial state, scheduled monument, world heritage site.

(Alphanumeric, unique, mandatory)

2.6.2. Date of designation or protection

The date on which the designation or protection was legally granted. Use of the ISO standard for date is recommended, for example, 1992-11-27.

(Alphanumeric, unique, optional)

2.6.3. Reference number

This records the designation or protection reference number, for example, SSSI47.

(Alphanumeric, unique, optional)

2.6.4. Originator of reference

The name of the individual or organisation responsible for the reference number, for example, National Museums Department. This field is mandatory if a reference number is used.

(Alphanumeric, unique, optional)

2.7. Archaeological summary

This optional section enables a brief free text description of the monument or site.

(Alphanumeric, unique, optional)

3. Glossary

This section contains the definitions of general terms used throughout the data standard.

Alphanumeric This indicates that the information to be entered may be made up of either alphabetical or numerical symbols, or a combination of them.

Cadastral A system for allocating reference numbers to blocks of land.

CIDOC The International Documentation Committee of ICOM.

Collection A body of archival material relating to a monument or site.

Designated site A site which has been identified as having a particular status by an organisation. It does not imply any legal protection.

Free text A text field, without a controlled vocabulary, which can be any length that is supported by the information system in use.

ICOM International Council of Museums.

ISO International Standards Organisation. An international organisation charged with developing standards for the international exchange of information.

Locality Any named inhabited area. Used in the core data standard for postal address where it is not the name of a town or city.

Mandatory Information that must be supplied ("unknown" may be an acceptable entry). In the core data standard, some sections are mandatory. Within sections that are optional, some sub-sections become mandatory if that section is used.

Monument An archaeological site with visible upstanding remains, for example, earthworks. Site is the more inclusive term.

Optional Information that need not be recorded either because it does not exist, or because it is inappropriate to the purposes of the recording organisation. Note that some optional sub-sections become mandatory if the optional sections containing them are used.

Originator of reference Used throughout the core data standard to identify individuals or organisations which are the source of references.

Parent-child relationship A hierarchical relationship between two items of data. The "parent" is one level above the "child". For a parent-child relationship, both the "parent" and the "child" must exist.

Provenance The place of origin of an object or record, or the documentation of the history of origin and transfer of objects or records.

Qualifier A term which modifies the principal term, providing additional information.

Site A particular location at which archaeological remains either exist or have been discovered in the past.

Site category A general classification system based on the site function. It includes one or more site types with a common function.

Site type A classification system that describes the function of the site. It is a more specific term than site category.

Topology The geometrical definition of a site or monument.

Unique Used in the core data standard to refer to a single piece of discrete information. Different or multiple pieces of discrete information are contained in separate, repeating fields.

4. Bibliography

Andresen, J. and Madsen, T., 1992: *Data Structures for Excavation Recording. A Case of Complex Information Management.* In Larsen (ed).

Council of Europe, 1993: *Architectural heritage: inventory and documentation methods in Europe.* Report of the Nantes Colloquy 1992, Cultural Heritage Series No. 28.

Council of Europe, 1995: *Core Data Index to Historic Buildings and Monuments of the Architectural Heritage*; Recommendation No. R (95) 3 of the Committee of Ministers of the Council of Europe to member states on co-ordinating documentation methods and systems related to historic buildings and monuments of the architectural heritage.

Grant, S.: *MONARCH: The Heritage Information System for England. Computer Applications and Quantitative Methods in Archaeology 1995.* BAR International Series.

International Council of Museums, International Committee for Documentation / Comité International pour la Documentation (CIDOC), 1992: *Normes Documentaires (Archéologie)/Data Standards (Archaeology).*

International Council of Museums, International Committee for Documentation / Comité International pour la Documentation (CIDOC), 1995: *International Guidelines for Museum Object Information: The CIDOC Information Categories.*

International Organisation for Standardization, 1988: *Specification for Representation of Dates and Times in Information Interchange.* ISO 8601:1988/BS EN 28601:1992. Geneva.

Lang, N. and Stead, S.D., 1992: *Sites and Monuments Records in England - Theory and Practice.* In Lock, G.and Moffett, J. (eds): *Computer Applications and Quantitative Methods in Archaeology 1991.* BAR International Series S 577, 69-76.

Larsen, C.U. (ed): *Sites and Monuments. National Archaeological Records.* The National Museum of Denmark, DKC, Copenhagen.

Marques, T. (ed), 1992: *Carta Arqueológica de Portugal.* Secretaria de Estado da Cultura e Instituto Português do Património Arquitectónico e Arqueológico.

Museums Services Division, 1993: *Humanities Data Dictionary of the Canadian Heritage Information Network.* Revised Edition.

Reilly, P. and Rahtz, S. (eds), 1992: *Archaeology in the Information Age. A Global Perspective*. One World Archaeology, vol 21. London.

Réseau Canadien d'Information sur le Patrimoine, 1994: *Dictionnaire de données des sciences humaines*.

Roberts, D.A. (ed), 1993: *European Museum Documentation Strategies and Standards*. Proceedings of an International Conference. The Museum Documentation Association.

Ross, S., Moffett, J. and Henderson, J. (eds), 1991: *Computing for Archaeologists*. Oxford University Committee for Archaeology Monograph 18.

Royal Commission on the Historical Monuments of England and Association of County Archaeological Officers, 1993: *Recording England's Past: A Data Standard for the Extended National Archaeological Record*. RCHME, London.

Royal Commission on the Historical Monuments of England and English Heritage, 1995: *Thesaurus of Monument Types: A Standard for Use in Archaeological and Architectural Records*. RCHME, Swindon.

Fiche d'indexation minimale pour les sites archéologiques

2. Fiche d'indexation minimale pour les sites archéologiques

Table des matières

Préface

Dans le cadre du programme du Conseil de l'Europe créé pour favoriser la mise en œuvre de la Convention européenne pour la protection du patrimoine architectural, une fiche minimale pour l'inventaire des monuments et des sites a été élaborée entre 1987 et 1992. A la suite de la signature de la Convention européenne révisée pour la protection du patrimoine archéologique (Malte, janvier 1992) et conformément à la Résolution n° 1 de la 3ᵉ Conférence des ministres responsables du patrimoine culturel, le Plan européen pour l'archéologie a été lancé en avril 1993 sous l'égide du Comité du patrimoine culturel du Conseil de l'Europe.

Un des cinq principaux éléments du Plan européen pour l'archéologie consistait en un programme axé sur l'inventaire, les techniques et les normes de documentation en matière de patrimoine archéologique. Parmi les actions principales de ce programme figurait l'élaboration d'une fiche minimale pour l'indexation des sites archéologiques, dans la lignée de celle établie pour le patrimoine architectural. Un petit groupe de travail fut alors constitué dans ce but.

Or, le Comité international pour la documentation (CIDOC) du Conseil international des musées (ICOM) était déjà en train de préparer une norme documentaire archéologique, suivant le modèle de la fiche d'indexation minimale pour le patrimoine architectural du Conseil de l'Europe. Le groupe de travail du Conseil de l'Europe estima alors que la façon d'agir la plus pragmatique était d'adopter la norme du CIDOC comme base de sa propre fiche minimale, sous réserve de quelques aménagements rendus nécessaires par la couverture géographique plus restreinte du Conseil de l'Europe. En réalité, cela implique peu de changements et la fiche minimale présentée ici est effectivement celle préparée par le CIDOC.

La fiche d'indexation minimale pour les sites archéologiques établie par le Conseil de l'Europe a été approuvée par plus de 100 représentants de 32 pays lors du colloque intitulé «Le patrimoine archéologique: normes relatives à l'inventaire et à la documentation en Europe», tenu à Oxford en septembre 1995.

Les personnes et les pays ayant participé aux activités du groupe de travail du Cidoc sur les sites archéologiques sont:

Veletta Canouts (Etats-Unis);
Nigel Clubb (Royaume-Uni);
Dominique Guillot (France);
Henrik Jarl Hansen (Danemark);
Roger Leech (Royaume-Uni);

Zana Kamberi (Albanie);
Judy Marsh (Canada);
Irina Oberlander-Tarnoveanu (Roumanie);
Andrzej Prinke (Pologne);
Gillian Quine (Royaume-Uni);
Trevor Reynolds (Royaume-Uni);
Stephen Stead (Royaume-Uni);
Elena Tashak (Russie).

Les personnes et les pays ayant participé aux activités du groupe de pilotage du Conseil de l'Europe sur les techniques de documentation en archéologie sont:

Comité de coordination:

Roger Leech (Royaume-Uni);
Charalambos Pennas (Grèce);
Willem Willems (Pays-Bas).

Membres du groupe de travail:

Martyn Barber (Royaume-Uni);
Rœl Brandt (Pays-Bas);
Dominique Guillot (France);
Henrik Jarl Hansen (Danemark);
Irina Oberlander-Tarnoveanu (Roumanie);
Jean François van Regteren Altena (Pays-Bas).

1. Introduction

1.1. Objectifs de la fiche d'indexation minimale

La documentation sur les sites archéologiques joue un rôle essentiel dans la compréhension, la conservation et la préservation du patrimoine archéologique. En Europe, une grande variété de méthodes d'enregistrement sont employées pour la réalisation des inventaires, souvent dans un cadre national. La réalisation de ces différents inventaires peut obéir à différentes raisons. Toutefois, certaines de ces raisons sont largement répandues, en particulier celles ayant trait à la protection du patrimoine archéologique et à la diffusion au public des informations. Le présent document a trois objectifs:

– faciliter la communication entre les organismes nationaux et internationaux responsables de l'inventaire et de la protection du patrimoine archéologique;

– aider les pays qui commencent à développer un système d'enregistrement pour l'inventaire et la protection du patrimoine archéologique;

– faciliter la recherche utilisant les données minimales dans des cas ayant une dimension internationale.

Dans la forme présentée ici, la fiche d'indexation minimale pour le patrimoine archéologique est très proche de celle préparée par le Conseil de l'Europe pour les monuments historiques et les édifices du patrimoine architectural (Conseil de l'Europe, 1995). Cela devrait intéresser les pays capables ou désireux d'inclure dans une seule base de données toutes les informations relatives au patrimoine bâti. De plus, cette norme peut être reliée à celle préparée par le CIDOC pour les objets archéologiques (CIDOC, 1992), ainsi qu'à la norme du CIDOC pour les objets muséographiques, qui concerne également les objets archéologiques (CIDOC, 1995).

1.2. Utilisation de la fiche d'indexation minimale

Les diverses sections représentent les catégories minimales d'information nécessaires pour documenter un site, que ce soit dans un but d'aménagement, de gestion, d'enseignement, ou autre. En outre, il peut être fait référence à d'autres informations contenues dans des bases de données, des centres de documentation ou autres lieux, qui peuvent être nécessaires à la connaissance détaillée et à la protection des sites individuels ou des grandes catégories de sites.

Les sections obligatoires de la norme constituent l'information minimale nécessaire pour décrire un site archéologique à l'aide de champs structurés indexés et de champs en texte libre. Les sections, sous-sections et champs facultatifs permettent un enregistrement plus détaillé. C'est ainsi qu'un site peut être relié à un ensemble dont il fait partie, ou aux enregistrements des fouilles dont il a été l'objet. Un renvoi peut aussi être fait à des informations documentaires plus détaillées détenues ou connues par l'organisme responsable de l'enregistrement. Le niveau d'enregistrement peut donc varier en fonction des besoins et des moyens de l'organisation.

Toutes les sections ne sont pas obligatoires. Chaque section contient un nombre variable de sous-sections, dont certaines sont obligatoires, c'est-à-dire que l'information doit être enregistrée; d'autres sont au contraire facultatives, et leur présence dépendra donc des priorités de l'organisme responsable de l'inventaire. L'information peut aussi ne pas exister. Par exemple, il peut très bien n'y avoir jamais eu de fouille sur un site, auquel cas la sous-section 2.1.8 ne sera pas remplie.

Même si beaucoup de sous-sections sont facultatives, dès lors qu'il a été décidé d'enregistrer l'information concernée, certains ou la totalité de leurs champs deviennent obligatoires. Par exemple, s'il est décidé d'indiquer des renvois vers des enregistrements d'opération de fouille (sous-section 2.1.8), alors il est obligatoire d'indiquer la référence de l'opération et le nom de l'organisation responsable de son enregistrement.

Les sections de la fiche d'indexation minimale sont ainsi organisées:

– la section 1 comprend l'identification et le nom du site, et permet les renvois vers des enregistrements d'opération, par exemple des fouilles ou des prospections, entreprises sur le site, et les enregistrements du mobilier et des archives du site;

– la section 2 permet de localiser le site à l'aide d'indications postales, politiques, cartographiques ou autres;

– la section 3 décrit le type du site;

– la section 4 permet d'indiquer la datation du site ou de ses phases d'utilisation;

– la section 5 contient l'état de conservation actuel du site;

– la section 6 permet de noter toute forme de protection, juridique ou autre, s'appliquant au site;

– la section 7 est un bref résumé des connaissances archéologiques sur le site.

Bien que beaucoup des champs ne nécessitent qu'une seule entrée (ils sont indiqués comme «monovaleur»), il est évident que, dans certains cas, plusieurs termes peuvent s'appliquer à un site à l'intérieur d'un même champ. Par exemple, un site peut s'étendre à cheval sur deux divisions administratives, ou plusieurs fouilles peuvent avoir eu lieu sur le même site. Dans ce cas, la norme recommande la répétition de la sous-section ou de la section entière, plutôt que la multiplication des champs. Ainsi, dans le cas de plusieurs opérations de fouille sur un même site, on traitera chacune d'entre elles séparément, en répétant à chaque fois toute la section 2.1.8.

1.3. Mise en œuvre de la fiche d'indexation minimale

La fiche d'indexation minimale a été replacée dans un cadre théorique, qui peut être valable aussi bien pour un système manuel que pour un système informatisé. Les organisations désireuses d'appliquer cette norme sont susceptibles d'utiliser l'un et l'autre pour répondre à leurs besoins spécifiques. Les concepts théoriques qui sous-tendent la fiche minimale sont expliqués en détail dans le document qui présente la norme documentaire du CIDOC, et ne sont qu'évoqués ici.

La nécessité de maintenir une relation étroite avec la fiche d'indexation minimale pour le patrimoine architectural a imposé des contraintes sur la forme et le contenu. Toutefois, la norme préparée par le CIDOC tient compte de l'expérience des institutions qui ont mis en œuvre des systèmes basés sur des principes similaires, comme DKC (Danemark), MONARCH (Angleterre), DRACAR (France) et ARCHIS (Pays-Bas).

Un élément important pour la fiche, mais également pour les bases de données archéologiques, est la manière dont les différentes sections sont liées. En clair, toutes les sections doivent être reliées à la section 2.1, qui identifie le site, l'origine et la date de l'enregistrement. En outre, d'autres sections doivent être liées entre elles. Par exemple, il est indispensable de lier très étroitement la section 2.3 (Type) et la section 2.4 (Datation), afin d'expliciter les sites multi-périodes ou ceux dont l'usage a changé au cours du temps, par exemple enceinte/âge du bronze, habitat ouvert/âge du fer, villa/gallo-romain.

1.4. L'avenir de la fiche d'indexation minimale

Cette fiche d'indexation minimale est conçue pour servir de guide. Dans des pays différents, les inventaires sont réalisés par diverses organisations, avec des objectifs différents, et portent sur des sites archéologiques caractéristiques de cultures ou de régions particulières. C'est pour cette raison que la plupart des rubriques indiquées ici sont facultatives plutôt qu'obligatoires, afin de permettre à chaque pays de ne les utiliser que si elles sont pertinentes pour les buts recherchés.

Le Conseil de l'Europe recueillera tous commentaires concernant cette fiche minimale, notamment de la part d'organismes l'ayant utilisée dans leur propre base de données patrimoniales. Le Conseil de l'Europe souhaite que sa fiche minimale reste identique à la norme établie par le CIDOC, sur laquelle elle a été fondée. En conséquence, le Conseil de l'Europe se propose de rester en relations avec le CIDOC pour les évolutions futures de la norme. Tous les commentaires reçus par le Conseil de l'Europe seront transmis au CIDOC pour étude, et le Conseil de l'Europe adoptera ensuite toute modification, applicable à l'Europe, qui serait occasionnée par ces commentaires.

1.5. Personne à contacter pour toute remarque

Dominique Guillot, ministère de la Culture, Direction du patrimoine, Sous-Direction de l'archéologie, 4 rue d'Aboukir, 75002 Paris, France.

2. Fiche d'indexation minimale

On trouvera ci-dessous la définition des sections, sous-sections et champs proposés dans la fiche minimale. Certaines rubriques sont obligatoires. D'autres sont facultatives et peuvent donc être ou non remplies, suivant la pertinence des informations disponibles et les objectifs poursuivis par chaque organisme ou institution.

2.1. Identification et nom du site

Section obligatoire, qui permet d'identifier le site.

2.1.1. Numéro d'identification

Numéro ou combinaison de caractères identifiant de manière univoque chaque site inventorié par l'organisation dans sa base de données, par exemple 615649.

(alphanumérique, monovaleur, obligatoire)

2.1.2. Nom du site

Texte libre permettant d'identifier le site par son nom ou son appellation usuelle, par exemple Grotte Chauvet.

(alphanumérique, monovaleur, facultatif)

2.1.3. Date de rédaction et date de dernière mise à jour

Sous-section permettant d'indiquer la date de rédaction de la fiche et sa date de dernière mise à jour.

2.1.3.1. Date de rédaction

Date à laquelle la fiche a été rédigée. L'usage de la norme ISO pour les dates est recommandé, par exemple 1986-06-22.

(alphanumérique, monovaleur, obligatoire)

2.1.3.2. Date de dernière mise à jour

Dernière date à laquelle l'enregistrement a été créé ou modifié. L'usage de la norme ISO pour les dates est recommandé, par exemple 1993-07-12.

(alphanumérique, monovaleur, obligatoire)

2.1.4. Producteur de la référence

Nom de la personne ou de l'organisme responsable de l'enregistrement. Cette information permet d'établir la provenance de chaque fiche lors des échanges de données, par exemple Royal Commission on the Historical Monuments of England.

(alphanumérique, monovaleur, obligatoire)

2.1.5. Renvoi à d'autres fiches du même fichier

Cette sous-section permet des renvois à d'autres fiches du même fichier, par exemple pour indiquer une relation entre un site individuel et un ensemble, comme entre une maison et un habitat. Elle est facultative, et peut être répétée autant que de besoin.

2.1.5.1. Numéro d'identification

Numéro ou combinaison de caractères identifiant de manière unique chaque enregistrement lié, par exemple SM97342.

(alphanumérique, monovaleur, obligatoire)

2.1.5.2. Type de la relation

Ce champ indique le type de relation entre fiches reliées, par exemple une relation hiérarchique de type «parent-enfant» reliant un complexe archéologique à un site individuel. Le qualificatif sera l'un des suivants: «fait partie de», «contient» ou «est en liaison avec». Dans le cas de l'enregistrement d'une maison, la relation à un habitat sera «fait partie de». Dans l'enregistrement de l'habitat, la relation à la maison sera «contient». La maison peut aussi avoir une relation «est en liaison» avec une autre maison appartenant au même groupe d'habitat.

(alphanumérique, monovaleur, obligatoire)

2.1.5.3. Producteur de la référence

Nom de la personne ou de l'organisme responsable de l'enregistrement, par exemple Sous-Direction de l'archéologie.

(alphanumérique, monovaleur, obligatoire)

2.1.6. Renvoi aux collections et aux objets archéologiques

Cette sous-section permet de faire référence aux collections archéologiques provenant du site. Elle est facultative, et peut être répétée autant que de besoin.

2.1.6.1. Numéro d'identification

Numéro ou combinaison de caractères identifiant de manière unique chaque collection ou objet relié au site, par exemple 57486.

(alphanumérique, monovaleur, obligatoire)

2.1.6.2. Producteur de la référence

Nom de la personne ou de l'organisme responsable de l'enregistrement, par exemple Musée des Antiquités Nationales.

(alphanumérique, monovaleur, obligatoire)

2.1.7. Renvoi à la documentation

Cette sous-section permet de faire référence aux sources documentaires, publiées ou non, associées au site. Elle est facultative, et peut être répétée autant que de besoin.

2.1.7.1. Numéro d'identification

Numéro ou combinaison de caractères identifiant de manière unique chaque document, par exemple DD27483.

(alphanumérique, monovaleur, obligatoire)

2.1.7.2. Type de document

Type de source associée au site. Un vocabulaire contrôlé est souhaitable, par exemple source photographique, graphique, écrite non publiée, bibliographique, électronique, cartographique.

(alphanumérique, monovaleur, obligatoire)

2.1.7.3. Producteur de la référence

Nom de la personne ou de l'organisme responsable de l'enregistrement de la documentation associée, par exemple Service régional de l'Inventaire Général.

(alphanumérique, monovaleur, obligatoire)

2.1.8. Renvoi à des opérations archéologiques

Cette sous-section permet de relier, par exemple, les fiches des opérations de fouille ou de relevés dont le site a fait l'objet. Lorsque plusieurs opérations ont eu lieu sur un même site, par exemple une prospection suivie d'une fouille, on remplira plusieurs entrées séparées. Cette sous-section est facultative, et peut être répétée autant que de besoin.

2.1.8.1. Numéro d'identification

Numéro ou combinaison de caractères identifiant de manière unique chaque enregistrement d'opération reliée au site, par exemple FP1995/6.

(alphanumérique, monovaleur, obligatoire)

2.1.8.2. Type d'opération

Nature de l'opération, par exemple fouille, prospection. Pour plusieurs opérations, utiliser des entrées séparées.

(alphanumérique, monovaleur, obligatoire)

2.1.8.3. Date de début de l'opération

Date à laquelle l'opération a commencé. L'usage de la norme ISO pour les dates est recommandé, par exemple 1896-06-04.

(alphanumérique, monovaleur, facultatif)

2.1.8.4. Date de fin de l'opération

Date à laquelle l'opération s'est terminée. L'usage de la norme ISO pour les dates est recommandé, par exemple 1896-07-30.

(alphanumérique, monovaleur, facultatif)

2.1.8.5. Producteur de la référence

Nom de la personne ou de l'organisme responsable de l'enregistrement de l'opération, par exemple Service des fouilles.

(alphanumérique, monovaleur, obligatoire)

2.2. Localisation

Cette section obligatoire définit la localisation spatiale du site à l'aide d'informations administratives, postales, géographiques et cartographiques.

Toute combinaison de sous-sections définies ci-dessous peut être utilisée pour identifier la localisation d'un site. Il est possible d'utiliser plusieurs types de sous-sections pour préciser la localisation. Il est à noter qu'il est obligatoire de renseigner au moins une sous-section, mais qu'aucune n'est obligatoire.

2.2.1. Localisation administrative

Sous-section facultative qui peut être répétée si besoin est.

2.2.1.1. Pays ou nation

Nom du pays ou de la nation où le site est situé, par exemple France.

(alphanumérique, monovaleur, facultatif [obligatoire pour l'échange de données entre pays])

2.2.1.2. Division géopolitique

A utiliser pour indiquer la division géographique ou politique du pays où le site est localisé, par exemple les régions en France, les *Länder* en Allemagne, les comtés en Grande-Bretagne.

(alphanumérique, monovaleur, obligatoire)

2.2.1.3. Subdivision administrative

A utiliser pour indiquer les autres subdivisions administratives dont relève le site. Selon la structure administrative de chaque pays, il peut être nécessaire d'indiquer plusieurs valeurs, comme en France où la région est divisée en départements, arrondissements, cantons et communes, par exemple Morbihan, Lorient, Quiberon, Carnac nécessiteraient quatre entrées.

(alphanumérique, monovaleur, obligatoire)

Il est à noter qu'il est essentiel de distinguer les différents niveaux de subdivisions administratives dont dépend le site, par exemple locales ou régionales.

2.2.2. Localisation du site

Sous-section facultative permettant une description en texte libre de la localisation du site.

2.2.2.1. Description de la localisation

Champ en texte libre permettant une courte description de la situation afin d'aider à l'identification sur le terrain et de fournir une localisation plus précise dans les territoires peu peuplés ou mal cartographiés.

(alphanumérique, monovaleur, obligatoire)

2.2.3. Adresse

Permet l'enregistrement de la localisation de site par une adresse, essentielle-
ment en milieu urbain. Cette sous-section est facultative et peut être répétée
si besoin est. Tous les champs sont facultatifs, mais au moins l'un d'entre eux
doit être renseigné.

2.2.3.1. Désignation postale

A utiliser pour l'adresse postale du site, par exemple Cruive Cottage.

(alphanumérique, monovaleur, facultatif)

2.2.3.2. Numéro dans la voie

A utiliser pour le numéro du site dans la rue, par exemple 27 *bis*.

(alphanumérique, monovaleur, facultatif)

2.2.3.3. Nom de la voie

A utiliser pour le nom de la rue, par exemple Calea Victoriei.

(alphanumérique, monovaleur, facultatif)

2.2.3.4. Localité

A utiliser pour les unités non administratives, comme les noms de hameaux
ou de lieux-dits, par exemple Pincevent.

(alphanumérique, monovaleur, facultatif)

2.2.3.5. Commune

A utiliser pour le nom de la ville ou du village, par exemple Stockholm.

(alphanumérique, monovaleur, facultatif)

2.2.3.6. Code postal, ou tout autre code national d'identification postale

Utiliser ce champ pour le code servant à l'adressage, par exemple 67000, K1A
OC8.

(alphanumérique, monovaleur, facultatif)

2.2.4. Références cadastrales

Certains pays utilisent un système attribuant des numéros à chaque parcelle de terrain. Les références des parcelles cadastrales contenant le site peuvent être indiquées ici. Cette sous-section est facultative et peut être répétée autant que de besoin.

2.2.4.1. Référence cadastrale

Permet le renvoi au système de numérotation des parcelles utilisé dans certains pays, par exemple 9417\278.

(alphanumérique, monovaleur, facultatif)

2.2.5. Références cartographiques

Sous-section facultative à utiliser pour indiquer en coordonnées cartésiennes la localisation spatiale du site par rapport au système de projection cartographique utilisé par le pays. Cette sous-section peut être répétée pour chaque série de coordonnées.

2.2.5.1. Identifiant

Identifiant de l'entité cartographique qui va être décrite, lorsque le site est formé de plusieurs entités de ce type. Par exemple polygone 1.

(alphanumérique, monovaleur, facultatif)

2.2.5.2. Système de référence utilisé

Par exemple UTM, Lambert, GPS, Ordnance Survey.

(alphanumérique, monovaleur, obligatoire)

2.2.5.3. Topologie

Indique si les coordonnées sont relatives à un point, une ligne ou une aire, par exemple P, L, A.

(alphanumérique, monovaleur, obligatoire)

2.2.5.4. Précision

Permet d'indiquer la précision et la fiabilité des coordonnées cartographiques. Un vocabulaire contrôlé est souhaitable, par exemple approximatives, centrées, etc.

(alphanumérique, monovaleur, obligatoire)

Les quatre champs suivants peuvent être répétés pour chaque coordonnée.

2.2.5.5. Numéro d'ordre

Lorsqu'un site archéologique est de forme linéaire ou polygonale, il peut être préférable d'entrer les coordonnées de plusieurs points plutôt que d'un seul, par exemple son point central. Ces points doivent alors être saisis dans l'ordre. C'est le numéro d'ordre du point qu'il faut indiquer ici pour chaque jeu de coordonnées, par exemple 1 pour un point, 1,2... pour une ligne, 1,2,3... pour un polygone.

(alphanumérique, monovaleur, obligatoire)

2.2.5.6. Coordonnée Z

Valeur ou identifiant de la coordonnée. Permet de localiser un site par rapport à un référentiel d'altitude, par exemple 250 mètres au-dessus du niveau N.G.F.

(alphanumérique, monovaleur, facultatif)

2.2.5.7. Coordonnée X

Valeur ou identifiant de la coordonnée, sur un axe est-ouest.

(numérique, monovaleur, obligatoire)

2.2.5.8. Coordonnée Y

Valeur ou identifiant de la coordonnée, sur un axe nord-sud.

(numérique, monovaleur, obligatoire)

2.3. Type

Cette section permet d'indexer un site à l'aide de critères descriptifs ou fonctionnels. Une entrée au moins est obligatoire, et doit être liée à celles de la section 2.4 (Datation), par exemple villa/époque romaine. Un vocabulaire contrôlé est indispensable, comprenant le terme «inconnu». Cette section peut être répétée afin de rendre compte des changements survenus dans le temps.

2.3.1. Type du site

Terme d'indexation. Il s'agit normalement de l'interprétation de l'édifice par la fonction ou la forme, par exemple villa; ouvrage de terre linéaire. Un vocabulaire contrôlé est souhaitable.

(alphanumérique, monovaleur, obligatoire)

2.3.2. Catégorie du site

Grande catégorie fonctionnelle ou descriptive à laquelle le type appartient, par exemple habitat. Un vocabulaire contrôlé est souhaitable. En cas d'utilisation d'un thésaurus hiérarchisé, ce champ est facultatif.

(alphanumérique, monovaleur, facultatif)

2.4. Datation

Cette section obligatoire permet de donner des dates précises quand elles sont connues, ou des datations par intervalles ou périodes. Cette section peut être répétée. Toute entrée dans cette section doit être liée à une entrée dans la section 2.3.

La sous-section 2.4.1 est obligatoire, mais toute combinaison de sous-sections définies ci-dessous peut être utilisée pour préciser la datation d'un site.

2.4.1. Période culturelle

Sous-section obligatoire permettant l'indexation du site en fonction de la période culturelle à laquelle il appartient.

2.4.1.1. Période culturelle

Période culturelle à laquelle appartient le site ou une partie du site, par exemple néolithique. Un vocabulaire contrôlé est souhaitable, contenant le terme «inconnu».

(alphanumérique, monovaleur, obligatoire)

2.4.2. Siècle

Sous-section facultative permettant d'indiquer le siècle auquel le site, ou une partie du site, appartient.

2.4.2.1. Siècle

Ce champ ne convient que pour les sites des périodes historiques, par exemple 17ᵉ siècle.

(alphanumérique, monovaleur, obligatoire)

2.4.3. Intervalle de dates

Sous-section facultative permettant d'indiquer les dates d'occupation du site, ou bien une période d'activité humaine particulière sur le site.

2.4.3.1. Entre

La date la plus ancienne, par exemple 1640.

(alphanumérique, monovaleur, obligatoire)

2.4.3.2. Et

La date la plus récente, par exemple 1660.

(alphanumérique, monovaleur, obligatoire)

2.4.4. Datation absolue

Cette sous-section facultative permet d'indiquer une datation précise obtenue à l'aide de sources documentaires (archives, inscription), ou d'une méthode scientifique (radiocarbone, dendrochronologie, etc.).

2.4.4.1. Datation

Date absolue attribuée au site, par exemple 1580-1410 CAL BC (HAR-1234).

(alphanumérique, monovaleur, obligatoire)

2.4.4.2. Méthode

Permet d'indiquer par quelle méthode la datation a été attribuée au site, par exemple carbone 14, dendrochronologie. Un vocabulaire contrôlé est souhaitable.

(alphanumérique, monovaleur, obligatoire)

2.5. Etat de conservation

Cette section permet d'indiquer l'état de conservation physique du site et la date à laquelle cet état a été constaté. Elle est facultative et peut être répétée. Pour assurer un suivi de l'état de conservation du site, il peut être utile de conserver ces données dans le temps. Cela permettra de noter toute atteinte ou destruction du site. Il peut aussi être nécessaire, en fonction des missions de l'organisme, d'ajouter des champs concernant la gestion du site.

2.5.1. Etat de conservation

Ce champ rend compte de l'intégrité physique du site. Un vocabulaire contrôlé est souhaitable, par exemple intact, détruit, arasé, démoli, ruiné, remanié, restauré, etc.

(alphanumérique, monovaleur, obligatoire)

2.5.2. Date de vérification

Date à laquelle l'état a été constaté. Nous recommandons l'utilisation de la norme ISO pour les dates, par exemple 1994-10-27.

(alphanumérique, monovaleur, facultatif)

2.6. Protection juridique

Section facultative permettant de préciser si l'édifice est protégé ou inscrit sur une liste, et, si oui, le type de protection ou d'inscription, et la date à laquelle elle a été accordée. Cette section peut être répétée.

2.6.1. Type de protection

Indique le type de mesure de protection. Un vocabulaire contrôlé est souhaitable pour préciser le niveau de protection, par exemple classement monument historique, patrimoine mondial.

(alphanumérique, monovaleur, obligatoire)

2.6.2. Date de protection

Date à laquelle la protection a été légalement accordée. Nous recommandons l'utilisation de la norme ISO pour les dates, par exemple 1992-11-27.

(alphanumérique, monovaleur, facultatif)

2.6.3. Numéro d'identification

Numéro de référence de la mesure de protection, par exemple SSSI47.

(alphanumérique, monovaleur, facultatif)

2.6.4. Producteur de la référence

Nom de la personne ou de l'organisme responsable de l'enregistrement. Ce champ est obligatoire si un numéro d'identification est indiqué.

(alphanumérique, monovaleur, facultatif)

2.7. Commentaire archéologique

Cette section facultative permet une description rapide du site en texte libre.

(alphanumérique, monovaleur, facultatif)

3. Glossaire

On trouvera ici les définitions des termes généraux utilisés dans la fiche d'indexation minimale.

Alphanumérique Désigne un champ dans lequel l'information peut être entrée sous forme de caractères alphabétiques, de chiffres, ou d'une combinaison des deux.

Cadastre Système permettant d'allouer des numéros d'identification à des parcelles de terrain.

Catégorie du site Classification basée sur la fonction du site. Elle comprend en général plusieurs types de site ayant servi à la même fonction.

CIDOC Comité international pour la documentation de l'ICOM.

Collection Ensemble de matériel provenant d'un site archéologique.

Facultatif Indique que l'information peut être absente, soit parce qu'elle n'est pas connue, soit parce qu'elle n'a pas d'utilité pour les objectifs de l'organisation établissant l'inventaire. Il est à noter que certaines sous-sections facultatives peuvent devenir obligatoires dès lors que la section facultative à laquelle elles appartiennent est utilisée.

ICOM International Council of Museums, Conseil international des musées

ISO International Standards Organization, organisation internationale chargée d'élaborer des normes pour les échanges internationaux de données.

Localité Toute zone habitée ayant une appellation autre que celle de la commune.

Monovaleur Indique dans la fiche minimale un champ ne pouvant contenir qu'une seule information. Si besoin est, le champ peut être répété.

Obligatoire Indique que l'information doit être présente («inconnu» est accepté). Certaines sections sont obligatoires dans la fiche minimale. A partir du moment où une section facultative est utilisée, elle peut contenir des sous-sections obligatoires.

Producteur de la référence Personne ou organisme qui est à la source de la référence concernée.

Relation parent-enfant Relation hiérarchique entre deux éléments. Le «parent» est au niveau supérieur de l'«enfant». Les éléments «parent» et «enfant» doivent exister pour qu'une telle relation soit créée.

Site Tout lieu recelant ou ayant recelé des vestiges de l'activité humaine.

Site inscrit Site reconnu par une organisation comme ayant un statut particulier, donc, à ce titre, inscrit sur une liste. Cela n'implique pas de protection légale.

Texte libre Champ textuel sans vocabulaire contrôlé, qui peut être de n'importe quelle longueur et exploité par tout système d'information.

Topologie Délimitation d'un site archéologique à l'aide d'une figure géométrique.

Type de site Classification indiquant la fonction du site de manière plus spécifique que la catégorie.

4. Bibliographie

Andresen, J. and Madsen, T., 1992: *Data Structures for Excavation Recording. A Case of Complex Information Management.* In Larsen (éd).

Conseil de l'Europe, 1993: *Patrimoine architectural: méthodes d'inventaire et de documentation en Europe*: actes du colloque de Nantes, 1992, Série Patrimoine culturel n° 28.

Conseil de l'Europe, 1995: *Fiche d'indexation minimale des monuments historiques et des édifices du patrimoine architectural*: recommandation n° R (95) 3 du Comité des Ministres du Conseil de l'Europe aux Etats membres relative à la coordination des méthodes et des systèmes de documentation en matière de monuments historiques et d'édifices du patrimoine architectural.

Grant, S.: *MONARCH: The Heritage Information System for England. Computer Applications and Quantitative Methods in Archaeology 1995.* BAR International Series.

International Council of Museums, International Committee for Documentation / Comité International pour la Documentation (CIDOC), 1992: *Normes Documentaires (Archéologie)/Data Standards (Archaeology).*

International Council of Museums, International Committee for Documentation / Comité International pour la Documentation (CIDOC), 1995: *International Guidelines for Museum Object Information: The CIDOC Information Categories.*

International Organisation for Standardization, 1988: *Specification for Representation of Dates and Times in Information Interchange.* ISO 8601:1988/BS EN 28601:1992. Geneva.

Lang, N. and Stead, S.D., 1992: *Sites and Monuments Records in England - Theory and Practice.* In Lock, G.and Moffett, J. (éd.): *Computer Applications and Quantitative Methods in Archaeology 1991.* BAR International Series S 577, 69-76.

Larsen, C.U. (éd.): *Sites and Monuments. National Archaeological Records.* The National Museum of Denmark, DKC, Copenhagen.

Marques, T. (éd.), 1992: *Carta Arqueológica de Portugal.* Secretaria de Estado da Cultura e Instituto Português do Património Arquitectónico e Arqueológico.

Museums Services Division, 1993: *Humanities Data Dictionary of the Canadian Heritage Information Network*. Revised Edition.

Reilly, P. and Rahtz, S. (éd.), 1992: *Archaeology in the Information Age. A Global Perspective*. One World Archaeology, vol 21. London.

Réseau Canadien d'Information sur le Patrimoine, 1994: *Dictionnaire de données des sciences humaines*.

Roberts, D.A. (éd.), 1993: *European Museum Documentation Strategies and Standards*. Proceedings of an International Conference. The Museum Documentation Association.

Ross, S., Moffett, J. and Henderson, J. (éd.), 1991: *Computing for Archaeologists*. Oxford University Committee for Archaeology Monograph 18.

Royal Commission on the Historical Monuments of England and Association of County Archaeological Officers, 1993: *Recording England's Past: A Data Standard for the Extended National Archaeological Record*. RCHME, London.

Royal Commission on the Historical Monuments of England & English Heritage, 1995: *Thesaurus of Monument Types: A Standard for Use in Archaeological and Architectural Records*. RCHME, Swindon.

Sales agents for publications of the Council of Europe
Agents de vente des publications du Conseil de l'Europe

AUSTRALIA/AUSTRALIE
Hunter Publications, 58A, Gipps Street
AUS-3066 COLLINGWOOD, Victoria
Fax: (61) 33 9 419 7154
E-mail: Robd@mentis.com.au

AUSTRIA/AUTRICHE
Gerold und Co., Graben 31
A-1011 WIEN 1
Fax: (43) 1512 47 31 29
E-mail: buch@gerold.telecom.at

BELGIUM/BELGIQUE
La Librairie européenne SA
50, avenue A. Jonnart
B-1200 BRUXELLES 20
Fax: (32) 27 35 08 60
E-mail: info@libeurop.be

Jean de Lannoy
202, avenue du Roi
B-1060 BRUXELLES
Fax: (32) 25 38 08 41
E-mail: jean.de.lannoy@euronet.be

CANADA
Renouf Publishing Company Limited
5369 Chemin Canotek Road
CDN-OTTAWA, Ontario, K1J 9J3
Fax: (1) 613 745 76 60

CZECH REPUBLIC/RÉPUBLIQUE TCHÈQUE
USIS, Publication Service
Havelkova 22
CZ-130 00 Praha 3
Fax: (420) 2 242 21 484

DENMARK/DANEMARK
Munksgaard
Østergade 26A – Postbox 173
DK-1005 KØBENHAVN K
Fax: (45) 77 33 33 77
E-mail: direct@munksgaarddirect.dk

FINLAND/FINLANDE
Akateeminen Kirjakauppa
Keskuskatu 1, PO Box 218
FIN-00381 HELSINKI
Fax: (358) 9 121 44 50
E-mail: akatilaus@stockmann.fi

FRANCE
C.I.D.
131 boulevard Saint-Michel
F-75005 Paris
Fax: (33) 01 43 54 80 73
E-mail: lecarrer@msh-paris.fr

GERMANY/ALLEMAGNE
UNO Verlag
Proppelsdorfer Allee 55
D-53115 BONN
Fax: (49) 228 21 74 92
E-mail: unoverlag@aol.com

GREECE/GRÈCE
Librairie Kauffmann
Mavrokordatou 9
GR-ATHINAI 106 78
Fax: (30) 13 23 03 20

HUNGARY/HONGRIE
Euro Info Service/Magyarország
Margitsziget (Európa Ház),
H-1138 BUDAPEST
Fax: (361) 302 50 35
E-mail: euroinfo@mail.matav.hu

IRELAND/IRLANDE
Government Stationery Office
4-5 Harcourt Road
IRL-DUBLIN 2
Fax: (353) 14 75 27 60

ISRAEL/ISRAËL
ROY International
41 Mishmar Hayarden Street
PO Box 13056
IL-69865 TEL AVIV
Fax: (972) 3 648 60 39
E-mail: royil@netvision.net.il

ITALY/ITALIE
Libreria Commissionaria Sansoni
Via Duca di Calabria 1/1, CP 552
I-50125 FIRENZE
Fax: (39) 0 55 64 12 57
E-mail: licosa@ftbcc.it

MALTA/MALTE
L. Sapienza & Sons Ltd
26 Republic Street, PO Box 36
VALLETTA CMR 01
Fax: (356) 233 621

NETHERLANDS/PAYS-BAS
De Lindeboom Internationale Publikaties
PO Box 202
NL-7480 AE HAAKSBERGEN
Fax: (31) 53 572 92 96
E-mail: lindeboo@worldonline.nl

NORWAY/NORVÈGE
Akademika, A/S Universitetsbokhandel
PO Box 84, Blindern
N-0314 OSLO
Fax: (47) 23 12 24 10

POLAND/POLOGNE
Główna Księgarnia Naukowa im. B. Prusa
Krakowskie Przedmiescie 7
PL-00-068 WARSZAWA
Fax: (48) 22 26 64 49

PORTUGAL
Livraria Portugal
Rua do Carmo, 70
P-1200 LISBOA
Fax: (351) 13 47 02 64

SPAIN/ESPAGNE
Mundi-Prensa Libros SA
Castelló 37
E-28001 MADRID
Fax: (34) 915 75 39 98
E-mail: libreria@mundiprensa.es

SWITZERLAND/SUISSE
Buchhandlung Heinimann & Co.
Kirchgasse 17
CH-8001 ZÜRICH
Fax: (41) 12 51 14 81

BERSY
Route d'Uvrier 15
CH-1958 LIVRIER/SION
Fax: (41) 27 203 73 32

UNITED KINGDOM/ROYAUME-UNI
TSO (formerly HMSO)
51 Nine Elms Lane
GB-LONDON SW8 5DR
Fax: (44) 171 873 82 00
E-mail: denise.perkins@theso.co.uk

UNITED STATES and CANADA/
ÉTATS-UNIS et CANADA
Manhattan Publishing Company
468 Albany Post Road, PO Box 850
CROTON-ON-HUDSON, NY 10520, USA
Fax: (1) 914 271 58 56
E-mail: Info@manhattanpublishing.com

STRASBOURG
Librairie Kléber
Palais de l'Europe
F-67075 STRASBOURG Cedex
Fax: +33 (0)3 88 52 91 21

Council of Europe Publishing/Editions du Conseil de l'Europe
F-67075 Strasbourg Cedex
Tel. +33 (0)3 88 41 25 81 – Fax +33 (0)3 88 41 39 10
E-mail: publishing@coe.int – Website: http://book.coe.fr